Our Government

The U.S.
Supreme Court

by Muriel L. Dubois

Consultant:
Steven S. Smith
Kate M. Gregg Professor of Social Sciences
Washington University, St. Louis, Missouri

Capstone
press

Mankato, Minnesota

First Facts is published by Capstone Press,
151 Good Counsel Drive, P.O. Box 669, Mankato, Minnesota 56002.
www.capstonepress.com

Library of Congress Cataloging-in-Publication Data
Dubois, Muriel L.
    The U.S. Supreme Court / by Muriel L. Dubois
    p. cm.—(First facts. Our government)
    Includes bibliographical references and index.
    Summary: Introduces children to the Supreme Court, its justices and how it selects and
decides cases.
    ISBN 0-7368-2291-7 (hardcover)
    ISBN 0-7368-4693-X (paperback)
    1. United States Supreme Court—Juvenile literature. 2. Courts—United States
Juvenile literature. [1. United States Supreme Court. 2. Courts.] I. Smith, Steven S., 1953–
II. Title. III. Series.
KF8742.Z9D83 2004
347.73'26—dc21   2002156401

Editorial Credits
Christine Peterson, editor; Jennifer Schonborn, series and book designer; Jo Miller, photo
    researcher; Eric Kudalis, product planning editor

Photo Credits
Corbis/Kim Kulish, 5; Franklin McMahon, 16–17; Bettmann, 20
Digital Stock, 7
Folio Inc./Rob Crandall, 9
Getty Images/Liasion/John Chiasson, 15; Alex Wong, 19
North Wind Picture Archives, 12–13
PhotoSpin, cover, 11

1 2 3 4 5 6 08 07 06 05 04 03

Table of Contents

People Have Rights

Police officers follow rules set by the U.S. Supreme Court. Officers arrest people who break laws. Supreme Court justices said officers must read these people their rights. Officers say, "You have the right to remain silent...." Supreme Court rules protect people's rights.

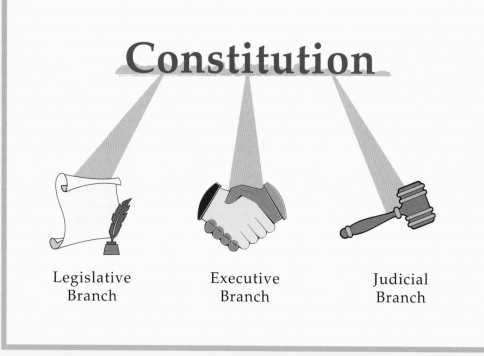

Constitution

Legislative Branch

Executive Branch

Judicial Branch

The U.S. government has three branches. The legislative branch passes bills that can become laws. The executive branch signs the bills into

 Fun Fact:

The Supreme Court met in the U.S Capitol until it received its own building in 1935.

new laws. The judicial branch explains the
U.S. Constitution and its laws. Courts make
up the judicial branch. The U.S. Supreme
Court is the country's highest court.

The Supreme Court Justices

In 1789, the first Supreme Court met with five justices. Today, nine justices serve on the Supreme Court. The chief justice leads the court. Justices serve on the court for life or until they retire. The president then chooses a new justice. The Senate votes on the president's choice for a new justice.

 Fun Fact:
Since 1800, Supreme Court justices have worn long black robes while serving the court.

Justices Hear Cases

The Supreme Court hears cases about laws and the U.S. Constitution. Justices listen to the facts about each case and then make a decision. Justices are asked to decide thousands of cases. They choose about 100 cases to decide each year.

 Fun Fact:
The Supreme Court was set up two years after the Constitution was signed in 1787.

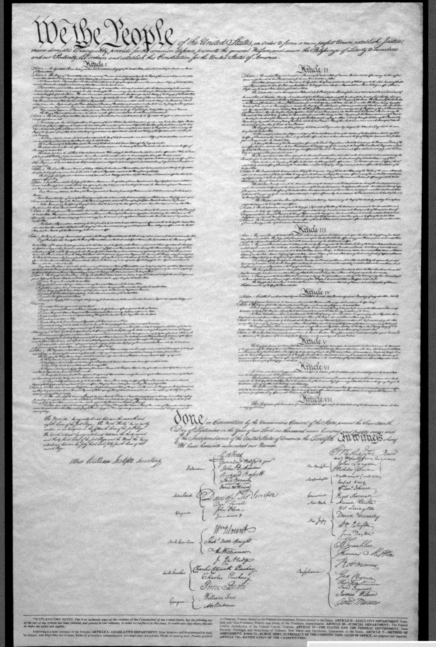

The U.S. Constitution

A Day in Court

The Supreme Court hears cases for nine months each year. The court meets three days a week. Justices hear four cases each day. Each case lasts one hour. For every case, justices write an opinion to explain the court's ruling.

 Fun Fact:
Cameras are not allowed in the Supreme Court. Artists may draw pictures of what happens in the courtroom.

13

Where a Case Begins

The Supreme Court hears cases that
were first decided by other courts.
A local or state court makes a ruling on
a case. People can ask to have that
ruling looked over by another court.
People also can ask the Supreme Court
to look over their cases.

A Case Goes to Court

In most courts, lawyers ask people questions to explain a case. A judge or jury listens to people tell their stories. The judge or jury then makes a decision. In the Supreme Court, only lawyers talk about the case. Justices ask questions. No jury is used. The justices decide the case.

Fun Fact:
The Chief Justice of the Supreme Court always sits in the middle chair.

The Justices Decide

Justices meet in private to talk about a case. Then they vote on a ruling. At least five justices must agree with the ruling. One justice writes the court's opinion. Justices also may write why they do not agree with the ruling. The Supreme Court's decision is final.

Amazing But True!

The U.S. Supreme Court ruled that all children should have an equal education. In 1954, third-grader Linda Brown had to go to a school that was only for African American children. There was a school for white students that was closer to Linda's home. The justices ruled African American children should not have to go to separate schools.

Hands On: Quill Pens

The first Supreme Court justices wrote their decisions with quill pens. Quill pens are still placed on tables in the Supreme Court. Try writing with a quill pen.

What You Need

An adult to help
Scissors
Large craft feathers
Washable paint or ink

Paper cups
Paper towels
Paper

What You Do

1. Have an adult use the scissors to cut the tip of a feather at an angle. The feather should be hollow so the ink or paint can get inside.
2. Have an adult cut a small thin line about .25 inch (.65 centimeter) long down the middle of the feather's tip.
3. Pour a small amount of paint or ink into a paper cup.
4. Dip the tip of the feather into the paint or ink. Use a paper towel to soak up any extra paint or ink from the pen.
5. Begin writing on a piece of paper.

Glossary

arrest (uh–REST)—to stop someone by law

case (KAYSS)—a legal problem settled in court

judicial (joo–DISH–uhl)—the branch of the government that explains laws

justice (JUHSS–tiss)—a member of the U.S. Supreme Court

opinion (uh–PIN–yuhn)—a report by a judge or jury giving the legal reasons for a court's ruling

right (RITE)—what the law says people can have or do

ruling (ROO–ling)—a decision made by a court

Senate (SEN–it)—one of the two houses of Congress that makes laws

Read More

Cornelius, Kay. *The Supreme Court*. Your Government–How it Works. Philadelphia: Chelsea House Publishers, 2000.

McElroy, Lisa Tucker (with help from Courtney O'Connor). *Meet my Grandmother: She's a Supreme Court Justice*. Grandmothers at Work. Brookfield, Conn.: Millbrook Press, 1999.

Internet Sites

Do you want to find out more about the U.S. Supreme Court? Let FactHound, our fact-finding hound dog, do the research for you!

Here's how:
1) Go to *http://www.facthound.com*
2) Type in the **Book ID** number: **0736822917**
3) Click on **FETCH IT**.

FactHound will fetch Internet sites picked by our editors just for you!

Index